GREECE

LAND OF GOLDEN LIGHT

By JANE WERNER WATSON

GARRARD PUBLISHING COMPANY   CHAMPAIGN, ILLINOIS

Acknowledgments

The author and publisher are grateful to Mrs. Katie Myrivili, Cultural Assistant, USIS, Athens, Greece, for checking the accuracy of the manuscript, and to Miss Helen Perry Doak, formerly Curriculum Consultant, Los Angeles County Board of Education, for checking educational concepts.

The author and publisher are indebted to Mrs. Alan J. B. Wace for permission to use in condensed form "The Legend of St. Cassianus," which appears in "Greece Untrodden," a collection of stories by Mrs. Wace's husband, the late eminent British archaeologist. They are grateful to Mrs. Wace and to *Archaeology Magazine* for permission to use in "The Gold Ring of Uncle Petros" the mythological theme of "The Golden Ring," another of Professor Wace's stories, which first appeared in *Archaeology Magazine*.

The illustrations for the book are by Spyros Vasiliou, one of Greece's most outstanding painters and leading designer of theatrical sets.

Photo credits

National Tourist Organization of Greece and: Nick Mavroyenis, 3; D. A. Harissiadis, 31 and 74; Nikos Kontos, 75; Raphaelidis, 90. Other photographs are by the author.

Cover art by Spyros Vasiliou

Endsheet maps by James Bier

BULGARIA
Black Sea
Byzantium
(Constantinople)
Istanbul
Sea of Marmara
Troy
Decherd Public School
Library
Decherd, Tennessee
N
W E
S
Aegean
Sea
TURKEY
Izmir
Chios
Stefanos'
home
ancient Ionian cities
Aleco's
holiday island
Kos
Rhodes
Sea of Crete
Knossos
Crete
0 50 100 150
miles

GREECE: LAND OF GOLDEN LIGHT

leads us through the rugged mountains and over the busy sea lanes of a land whose ancient past is a part of our heritage. The Greece of today is much less familiar to most of us, and it is this living land we come to know in this book.

We watch the slow turn of the year in a mountain village, and taste the flavor of life in a seaside town. We vacation with a city family on an Aegean island, and watch the surge of activity in busy Athens. The stories, which take us into the lives of young Greeks, are illustrated with true Greek flavor by one of Athens' outstanding painters and theatrical designers, Spyros Vasiliou.

Factual chapters present the geography, occupations, transportation, history, educational framework, traditions, and government of Greece in a lively fashion which brings to social studies new breadth and intimacy.

Pictures by Greek artist Spyros Vasiliou

Contents

I. The Gold Ring
of Uncle Petros

The Homecoming

Not if he lived to be a hundred would Stefanos forget the night when his great-uncle Petros came home—nor all that followed.

Stefanos had been half asleep on a heap of fish nets in his father's boat when the Athens steamer came gliding slowly over the dark waters, its siren hooting hoarsely.

The ship's anchor went down with a grating rattle of the long chain. Lamp lights blossomed down the long quay. Dark shadowy figures ran about, crossing the circles of light, then blending into the shadows again. Voices called.

Stefanos had just sat up, shivering in the night chill, when his father jumped down from the seawall into the boat. Soon the lantern at the prow of their small boat burst into golden light. With a creak of oars, the boat leaped across the water toward the steamer's side.

Now lights danced all up and down the length of the ship towering over them. On the high deck figures raced about, and the heavy tread of feet could be heard. More voices shouted.

Stefanos' father stood up and shouted back through cupped hands. Down came a rope sling. Up went their boatload of vegetables and fruits.

Then out of the night roared a new voice.

"Is there anyone here named Kapasousis? Any son of the house of old Stefanos Kapasousis?"

Stefanos felt a prickling of his skin at the sound of his own name across the darkness.

"I am Stefanos Kapasousis!" he called.

"Who asks?" his father added.

"Who indeed but Petros Kapasousis himself, home from the seven seas after more years of wandering than Odysseus!"

"Uncle Petros!" cried Father. "Welcome! I will row to the ladder and take you aboard."

Before Stefanos could rub his eyes the boat was dipping and bobbing under the weight of a dark, stocky figure. This half-seen stranger, clasping Father in a big hug, was the great-uncle Petros whom Stefanos had heard about all his life!

Soon it was young Stefanos' turn to be swept off his feet. His face became buried in the thick wool of a seaman's jacket that smelled richly of salt water and tobacco and distant lands.

Cold metal touched Stefanos' forehead; he reached up and found his hand clasping a gold ring. The ring swung from a woolen string around Uncle Petros' neck.

"What is this?" Stefanos asked.

"That?" said Uncle Petros, his big hand taking the ring gently from Stefanos' grasp. "That is my lucky piece. I will tell you the tale of it soon enough, for it lies back of the whole story of my life. But heads up, lads! Here's my gear!"

Down into the boat swung a bulging duffel bag and a suitcase tied with twine.

"Let me try my hand at an oar, lad," Uncle Petros said as he elbowed Father aside. Stefanos smiled to himself to hear his father called "lad."

Then over the water they sped, and soon they were bumping the old rubber tires that cushioned the seawall.

"I will get a donkey," said Father, "to carry your bundles home and a second one for you to ride, Uncle. It is a long walk up into the hills to the village."

"Donkeys!" cried Uncle Petros. "This is a rare thing, this homecoming. We shall have a taxi!"

His shout soon brought the town's one taxi.

Yanni, the driver, jumped out, grinning proudly. He opened the back door and waved a feather duster over the seats as if it were a magic wand.

"So this is your taxi," said Uncle Petros with a smile. "If only I could show you the big, fast cars of Rio and Hoboken and other ports!"

He flung his luggage up onto the roof of the taxi, and Yanni tied it on with twine. Then Father and Uncle Petros and Stefanos all climbed into the back seat.

A light shone inside the taxi to welcome them.

Stefanos looked at the bright rug on the floor. They were sitting on another fine rug with a big orange tiger in its design, which had been spread on the back seat. Stefanos could not see how the cars in Rio and Hoboken could be finer.

"Let us stop at the *taverna* in the village," said Uncle Petros. "It is too late for your womenfolk to cook supper for us. How long it has been since I have tasted octopus beaten tender on the island rocks! And good white cheese from the milk of island goats!"

The taxi drew up before the taverna with a fine screeching of brakes. There were only two men in the taverna's whitewashed courtyard. They were sitting over a backgammon board. But word of Petros' homecoming soon spread.

One after another the men of the village trooped in. Some looked as though they had been asleep. But they pulled up their chairs in a circle around the table of Uncle Petros. The waiter hurried back and forth, bringing small plates with rounds of octopus, hot from the grill, slices of sweet onion, pieces of hardboiled egg, chunks of white cheese.

"Forty years you have been away, Petros?"

asked one of the old men who came up to greet him. "I myself was for 22 years in Boston, Massachussetts. I sold fruits and vegetables. How the ladies loved to trade with me!"

"Hush, Stanos," broke in another man. "We have all heard about your years away. This is Petros' homecoming. Tell us about your travels, Petros, old friend."

"Oh, where to start!" groaned Petros, shaking his head. "What shall I tell you first?"

"I know," Stefanos put in shyly. "Start with the story of the gold ring you wear around your neck."

So Uncle Petros did.

The Story of the Ring

"You see this ring of thick old gold," said Uncle Petros, "and you may wonder why I wear it around my neck on this dirty string. You will be surprised when I tell you I think my life depends on it." And this is the story Uncle Petros told.

It was the morning long ago, when I was leaving home to go off to sea. As I walked down the road, I met some shepherd families moving with their flocks up to high pastures.

Behind the flocks came three old women who were spinning wool as they walked along. I bowed to the grandmothers, and one of them

called to me. When I stopped, she handed me
this ring. As you see it is not very beautiful, so
I handed it back. She held up her hand and
shook her head, saying I was to keep it.

I showed her that it would not go on my
finger. You see it is not very large. The second
old woman measured off a length of the yarn
she was spinning and slipped the ring onto it.
The third old woman took a pair of scissors that
hung from her belt and snipped off the yarn.

The first woman then knotted it into a loop
and slipped it over my head.

"Don't lose it," she said.

"Don't sell it," cautioned the second.

"Don't cut it," said the third.

I looked down for a moment at the gold ring
dangling against my chest. Then I looked up to
thank the old women, but they were gone. I
called and looked among the rocks beside the
road. But they were nowhere to be seen.

Well, I wasted little thought on the strangeness
of that. Soon I was down at the port, saying
my farewells. I shipped out on the first small
ship, a *caique* (ka-eek') bound for Athens.

There I was lucky to find a freighter that

needed another deckhand. The ship was bound for America, carrying a load of tobacco. I signed on, and so I started my forty years of wandering.

The night watch can be lonely at sea. I soon found that this gold ring made good company. I could touch it and see this village as clearly as day, the house of my father, and even this taverna, lively with good talk.

I first guessed the real power of the ring when another sailor tried to take it away from me. He was a big, tough man, a head taller than I. His voice was a growl. His hand was heavy. He was always ready for a fight.

One night he made fun of me over the ring. He said only a woman would wear it so, around the neck. I could not take that. So we fought.

It was going badly for me. He was so much bigger, and the winner of many fights. Then he ripped the ring from my neck, tearing the yarn.

At that moment the ship pitched, and he lost his footing. The ring spun from his hand to the deck. The sailor reeled back against the rail and pitched over it into the sea.

Someone sounded the alarm, "Man overboard!" Someone else threw a life preserver. The engines

14

were reversed. A search went on, but no sign of him was to be seen.

Later, I found the ring in a coil of rope. I made a new knot in the torn yarn and slipped it over my head again. No one joked with me about it after that night.

This ring and I have been in ports in many a land since then. We have crossed every sea on earth, I think. We have sailed on rusty old freighters, on smelly oil tankers. We have polished the teak deck of the most beautiful ship on earth, the yacht of a rich Greek shipowner.

Back to the ring! Well, you meet all kinds of men at sea. Some have been many years at school and have read hundreds of books. But a fever in their blood makes them wanderers. Such a man became a friend of mine.

It was during the big war. I was on an oil tanker that was torpedoed. We had to jump into a sea of flaming oil. Many men died. I swam underwater as long as I could. When I came up, there was a boat nearby. Men pulled me into it. I was still gasping, but I saw that they were the enemy. I was a prisoner!

One of the men was a giant with yellow hair.

He saw my ring on its length of watersoaked yarn. He tried to yank it off. But the wet yarn would not break.

In that moment I heard the whine of a shell. The boat was struck and quickly sank beneath us. The water closed over my head. I swam away from that spot with all my strength.

Soon the spotlight of a British ship picked me out. The crew rescued me, but they found no trace of the enemy boat or any of its crew.

It was after that rescue that I met my friend. One night I told him the story of the ring.

He looked at it closely, but would not let me take it off to put it into his hands.

"Oh, no, old fellow," he said. "I don't want those three grandmothers after me! You know who they were? They were the three Fates—the Three Sisters of old legends. One spins the thread of our lives, the second measures it out, and the third snips it off when our appointed time has come."

I had to admit that I had not heard of these Three Sisters. We did not have a school in the village when I was a boy. We did not learn about the rich tales of our own land.

After that, my friend whiled away many an hour telling me wonderful tales of our own people of long ago. He told me about the old gods—Zeus who made the thunder roll, and Hera his sharp-tongued wife. He told about Apollo who drove the chariot of the sun across the sky, and about his sister Artemis, goddess of the moon. He told of the arrows of sickness those two shot from their bows to strike down men on earth.

I was sorry when a wireless came for him and called him away. But I have never forgotten him. I have never forgotten what he told me of the Three Sisters who measured the thread of my Fate and fastened it to my gold ring.

The Last of the Ring

By the time Uncle Petros finished his story of the ring, Stefanos was nodding in his chair. The men of the village looked at the ring with respect. They clapped Uncle Petros on the shoulder before they wandered home.

The days were rich for Stefanos after that. He was with his Uncle Petros most of the time, since school was on holiday. Together they walked every path on the island, visited every village. They sat around the tables of every taverna, Uncle Petros exchanging tales with the village men.

When they had seen all the island, Uncle Petros became restless. He seemed sad.

"I cannot stay long," he said.

One day when Father could go with them, they went up the highest hill of the island. Uncle Petros wanted to visit once again the old, old temple on the hilltop.

It was a hard, hot climb up a steep goat path. When they reached the top, Uncle Petros looked very tired. He mopped his face with a handkerchief. He walked slowly to a fallen pillar and sat down, leaning back against a tree trunk.

"We Greeks have never had much peace," he said. "Even the men who built this temple did not have peace. But they had glorious times." He smiled.

"I have had glorious times, too," he said. He looked far off across the hills, to where the sea glittered. Then he closed his eyes.

Stefanos thought Uncle Petros looked very ill. He ran off to get his father, who had stopped to visit with a friend in a field below. As he ran, he almost bumped into three old women who stood on the path looking up at the old temple.

They were talking among themselves. They were dressed like shepherd women. All three were spinning, as country women often do. One wore at her waist a pair of scissors, the blades glinting in the sun.

Stefanos darted around the three and found his father, still talking with his friend.

"Come quickly," he said. "Uncle Petros is sick, I think."

They hurried back to the temple. Uncle Petros still sat there, but he seemed to be asleep. His head drooped forward on his chest.

Father put his arm around Stefanos' shoulders.

"He has left us, Stefanos, as he said he must. And he has left just as he would have wished."

Stefanos was looking at Uncle Petros' throat.

"The ring!" he cried. "His gold ring is gone, yarn and all!"

Then he remembered the three women who were spinning. But they were nowhere to be seen.

2. This Is Greece

Imagine a rough square on the endsheet map of the eastern Mediterranean Sea. The northern boundary will run east from the Ionian Sea at the island of Corfu. As this line zigzags slightly northward, it crosses to a point above the coast of Asia Minor.

The eastern boundary is a shaky line off the coast of Asia Minor. The offshore islands will be included in your square, as well as the island of Rhodes.

The southern boundary cuts across open water. It will include the island of Crete. On the west,

the line will run north through water that flows
from the Mediterranean into the Ionian Sea.

None of these boundary lines will be perfectly
straight. The whole square will be tilted up a
bit to the northeast. Its bottom line will sag to
the south. But within it will lie Greece.

"This is more than half water!" you may say.
"There is more sea than land."

True enough. That is Greece! It is made up
of mountain ranges, half-drowned beneath the
slow rise of the Mediterranean Sea through the
ages. Four-fifths of the land of Greece lies on
mountain slopes.

The principal ranges run generally from the
northwest to the southeast. In the west, the coast
rises sharply from the sea. Toward the east, the
land slopes more gently to the water.

You can trace the bony fingers of the undersea
mountains far out from shore. Their peaks poke
up like knuckle bones through the waters of the
Aegean Sea. These islands lie so close together
that they made stepping stones for early sailors.
The men liked to come ashore each night. They
could sail the Aegean Sea with some land in
sight almost all the time.

On the mainland of Greece, the waters have crept far up the valleys between ranges, forming many gulfs and bays. The land pokes out between them in headlands and peninsulas.

One of the largest gulfs, the Gulf of Corinth, does not fit into this pattern. It slashes straight across the bony "hand" of Greece from west to east. South of the Gulf, the land known as the Peloponnesus (pel-a-pun-nee'-sus) is almost cut off. Even the narrow isthmus of land that connects it to the main body of Greece is cut by the man-made Corinth Canal.

Most Greeks have always lived on some island or headland or bay, not far from the sea. They have been cut off by mountains from neighbors who are really only a few miles away. These mountains rise up between towns, making roads hard to build and land travel difficult. The easiest road is the sea.

The Greeks thus became a seafaring people, sailing in their black ships over the wind-tossed waters. They also became a people divided into small city-states, each proud and independent. Geography made them so—the harsh, barren mountains and the broad, open sea.

At Cape Sunion Greek sailors of old built a temple to
Poseidon, god of the sea. It pointed the way to Athens.

Travel by Sea

Today the sea is still the best route for travel
and shipping in Greece. This small country has
one of the largest merchant fleets in the world.
Its ships travel from port to port all over the
world. Sometimes they carry goods from the
harbors of Greece.

Thessalonike, the second city of Greece, has a

very busy harbor. Athens, of course, has a harbor, too, but it is in a separate city, Piraeus (Pie-ree'-us). Piraeus used to be several miles away from Athens, but since people have been crowding into the cities, the two have grown so that there is no open space left between them. Together, Athens and Piraeus house almost a quarter of Greece's population.

Ships from all over the world crowd the harbor of Piraeus. In among them dart the sturdy, small steamers of the busy coastal and inter-island trade.

Food and clothing and most goods used by the people of the islands go through the port of

Ships of many lands visit the modern harbor of Piraeus. Many small island steamers dock here too.

Piraeus. Island crops travel to market on the same ships when they come back on their return journeys.

Travel by these small steamers is very lively. There are a few small cabins, but most passengers carry their own food and blankets and pay only for deck passage. They settle themselves in the open air with their baskets and bedrolls, their hampers of vegetables, bundles of cordwood, huge loaves of bread, cantaloupes and watermelons and tomatoes for market.

There may be sheep, dogs, pigs, goats, or even automobiles on these island steamers. Perhaps someone has a few chickens or turkeys, their legs tied together with twine. A rooster may complain loudly of this treatment.

Someone is sure to have a mandolin or guitar. Someone else is ready to sing. So the trip is never dull. And when the ship docks, the streets of the port city are full of life and noise.

Travel by Land

From Piraeus it is possible to take a small train north for the short journey to Athens. There is some train travel by regular railroads both to the north and south of the country. The railroads are rather slow, though, and not very modern. There are different widths of track, and not many miles of it in all.

If a trip is fairly short, a bus may be the handiest way to travel. Buses are found on all the roads of Greece, although five out of six miles of these roads are still not paved. They twist and turn up mountain slopes where only goats used to be able to go. The skillful bus drivers do not mind.

Stone bridges scarcely any wider than the bus connect the roads across deep gorges. There are no railings at the sides, but the passengers are not bothered. Once they have their bundles and baskets tied onto the bus roof, they relax. There is always someone to talk to. If you do not find an old friend, you talk to a stranger and make a new friend.

Sometimes the bus breaks down. Then everyone climbs out from the bus and offers suggestions to the driver and his helper. As they work flat on their backs under the bus or bent over the motor, you can imagine how delighted they are to have so much advice.

For a very short journey, a villager will probably go by donkey. For a long journey, he may fly. Airplane service connects many towns and cities that were once a lifetime apart. Fares are low on the airline run by the government. Planes are bringing distant mountain farms close to the heart of Greece.

Grove and Field

The farms of Greece were not very rich even in the earliest times. A handful of olives, a bit of grain, fruit in its season—these were the Greek foods of long ago. When a young bullock was offered to the gods, there was meat roasted on a spit. Some wine from the grapes grown on the hillsides was mixed with cool water from a spring among the rocks.

Time has not made the fields more fertile. Most of the crops of Greece are grown in the mountain valleys. Soil from the mountains has been washed down the rocky slopes into these valleys for hundreds and hundreds of years. Crops grow well in this soil, but most of the valleys are small.

In northern Greece, the mountains are highest

Olive trees line this road far south in the Peloponnesus.

and the plains are the widest. Here are broad fields, yellow with grain and green with tobacco. Many fields are small terraces built up by hand on the hillsides behind stone walls.

More than half of the people still work on the land. Their family farms average five to ten acres.

In the last 40 years, marshes have been drained to make new fields, and water has been brought to some dry areas. Better vines have been planted for grapes. New kinds of seeds have grown better crops of grain. New varieties of tobacco grow better quality leaves. Crops new to Greece, such as potatoes, beans and peas, rice, cotton, and sugar beets have been tried with success.

Even the new crops raised for sale cannot bring much money to farmers who have only four or five acres on which to raise them.

More than two-thirds of the land of Greece is so rocky and steep that no crops can be grown on it. A few goats scamper over the rocks, foraging for food. They have nibbled the shoots of young trees so hungrily that the trees have died, leaving many slopes bare.

Goats alone are not to blame for the lack of trees. The pines of old Greece gave long, straight timbers for shipbuilding. The traders and pirates of olden times needed many wooden ships, so pines were slashed down until slopes were left treeless.

Many cypress trees were cut to make furniture. When trees were cut for the cabinetmakers or shipbuilders, no one thought of planting more. Only in recent years has any replanting been done. Some day, more clumps of pines will

New varieties of plants and new irrigation systems are increasing production in fields of northern Greece.

whisper in the wind on the hillsides of Greece.

Olive and fruit trees have been tended for many hundreds of years. The soft gray-green of olive leaves and the twisted, gnarled trunks of old groves are a familiar sight. Olive oil is used for cooking, and small, bitter black olives are a favorite food. There are still many olives left to be shipped abroad. They are the third most important export ranking next to tobacco and grapes.

Many fruit trees send their roots deep into rocky soil to produce sweet fruits—apples, peaches, small hard pears, soft sweet figs, plums, and mulberries whose leaves feed silkworms. There are vines, too, some growing melons, while others grow grapes of all kinds and sizes.

In the late summer, the sun bakes the earth. Paths are powder-dry, roads swirl with dust. It is then that the figs begin to burst their thin skins, and the grapes droop in heavy clusters on the low vines.

Women slash off the bunches with long slender knives. Each bunch is laid gently in a basket. When the basket is full, a woman carries it on her shoulder out of the vineyard.

Wine grapes may be stamped by foot in a vat until the juice runs out. Small, round currant grapes are spread out on clean-swept ground or on racks or canvas. When the sun has dried

Baskets of grapes are ready to be carried to the wine vats here on the Aegean island of Samos.

The grape harvest brings a holiday for all the family, with singing and dancing to lighten work.

them to sweet, wrinkled raisins, they are packed into boxes. Trains of mules and donkeys wind down the twisting paths to the nearest harbor. From there the crop is shipped to market.

Much of the work on the small farms of Greece is still done in old-fashioned ways.

Grain, planted on the plains in February, is nourished by windy spring rains. By the time the summer sun has burned the green world to brown and gold, the grain is ripe.

Farmers build straw shelters in their fields. A whole family may move out from the nearby village and camp in the fields to guard the ripening crop. All of them help with the reaping.

The sheaves are spread on a round threshing floor that is plastered or is paved with smooth stones. Mules pull a small wooden platform round and round the floor. The movement of the platform rubs the grain loose from the husks. To make the platform heavier, members of the family take turns riding it. When the mother rides, her youngest hops aboard too, clinging to her legs as the mules amble slowly round and round.

As the stacks of grain grow, the winnowing begins. Wooden forks fling the grain up into the breeze, and the chaff is blown away. Up piles the grain. In the nearby fields the sheep and goats graze among the stubble. From the groves of pines and olives on the mountain slopes nearby, insects shrill. From a neighboring field, voices call. A song may ring out, as the sunny harvest days draw to a close.

Day of Machines

On large farms today, harvesting machines clatter swiftly across the fields. In towns and cities, other machines roar and pound in factories.

Greece does not have as many factories as the countries of western Europe, but even small towns may have a tobacco business or a cloth mill. These employ mostly women.

More and more young men go off to the cities to find work, if they want to leave the farm. Many of the factories of Greece are in Athens, the capital, and in Thessalonike, the second city of Greece.

These factories supply most of the cloth and furniture and other goods the Greek people buy. They make enough silk cloth and process enough tobacco so that some can be sold abroad. The tobacco and silk, like much of the grain that Greece sells to other countries, is likely to go out from the excellent harbor of Thessalonike.

Greece sends many young workmen to other countries, too. If young men cannot find work they like in Greece, they travel overseas. So many men have gone to other lands that some people say that Greece will soon be short of workers. Even now, many villages find they have few young men left.

Like most countries of the world today, Greece finds cities growing at the expense of her villages.

Wild flowers sparkle in the carpet of meadow grass
during the brief Greek spring.

Whatever the Weather

Spring in Greece is green and sparkling. Spring
showers bring out wild flowers to gleam like
jewels among the rocks and the thin grasses of
the bare mountains. There are lily-like asphodels
—white, pink, and yellow. There are clumps of
deep yellow crocuses and wild irises blown by the
fresh breezes. Delicate white anemones bow on
slender stems.

But spring does not last long. By mid-May,
summer has come, and the showers stop. The sun
shines, hot and bright, drying the land. Most of
the spring green dries to gold or dusty brown.

When the breeze blows from the south, it brings hot, dry, scratchy air from the distant Sahara Desert. People feel nervous and irritable when this southern *sirocco* (sa-rock'-o) blows.

Sometimes the summer wind comes from the north. It feels fresh and cool. But to island people it often brings gray, cloudy days with stormy seas. Then the waves crash on the rocks, tossing fountains of spray and shaking the houses in nearby villages.

At night the wind thunders and shrieks. The fishing boats and motor-powered caiques stay in the harbor. Inter-island steamers pass by the

A summer storm shakes a Greek island port. The winds may paralyze sea traffic for a week at a time.

small ports. When the northern *meltemia* (mel-tay-me-a) blows, no supplies come in, and no crops go out to market.

Autumn brings a cooling of the sun's heat. Clouds may gather in the sky that was so blue and clear all summer long. Rains are always welcome after the dry heat.

Dull browns soon freshen to green again as a curtain of rain sweeps across rock faces and races down long-dry crevices. Streams come to life in their stony beds and swell into short-lived rivers. People almost dance for joy in villages on the plains.

Up in the mountains, rains are not such a treat. Shepherds herd their flocks into rocky caves for shelter and think of lowland pastures, since winter is coming.

On the islands and along the coastlines, even the winters are mild. In Athens, for example, winter days are bright. The nights, though, may have a bitter chill and the stars an icy glitter.

In northern Greece, where the plains rise to higher mountains, winters are cold and stormy, with a good deal of snow and bitter winds. Here and there among these high peaks, pockets of snow lie in shady hollows far into the late spring.

Men who go up to work in the high pine woods often tramp through snow. In the autumn they go there to cut firewood. In the spring they collect pine resin. First, they gash the bark of the pines. Then, they fasten cups below the gashes to catch the resin as it oozes down. This resin is used in varnishes, medicines, and to line wooden wine casks. It gives a special flavor to the wine of Greece, as the climate and landscape give a special flavor to life in Greece.

In the spring men collect resin from the pine trees.

3. Life in Town and Village

Up from the shore rises the port town. Against the steep and rocky hillside, the houses look like children's blocks, square and flat-roofed. Many of these houses are whitewashed each year at Eastertime and perhaps again for Christmas, so they glitter and shine in the golden light of Greece. Other houses, yellow or grayish-blue or rose-red, are packed close together along narrow streets.

The streets are stone-paved, and some rise in stairsteps up the steep hillside. No cars can travel on those streets, but one may meet a donkey

Left: A churchyard on the island of Chios.

picking its way down the stairs while the bell on its necklace of blue clay beads tinkles gently with each step. The blue beads are for luck, and were once believed to protect the animal against "The Evil Eye." This is a custom left over from the days when the Turks ruled Greece.

Close to the waterfront, the shops of the village form a curving line. Doors and windows stand open to the street, for no one wants to be shut away from all the life outside.

In front of the shops, fruit is heaped in bright pyramids, shoes hang from lengths of twine, and sunlight sparkles on the shining scales of fresh-caught fish.

The waterfront is paved with smooth stones or concrete. Several small trees and some awnings shade patches of the pavement, while the rest is smoking hot in the sun.

Wooden tables stand in the shade. Rush-seated chairs are drawn up around the tables. There the men of the village spend their free time.

One may order a small cup of sweet, thick coffee by shouting to a man in the doorway of a café, but most of the time the men do not drink coffee or even smoke. They may watch two of their friends playing a game of backgammon on a patterned wooden board, or they may play a hand of cards. Most of the time they just talk.

Someone has a newspaper from Athens and he reads the news of the government aloud. Before he can finish an item, voices rise, hands wave, and a great argument begins. The men of Greece love to talk, to discuss, to argue, to use their wits against one another.

"A man who takes no interest in public affairs is considered a useless character," said a great leader of Athens 2,500 years ago. It is still true today.

The fruit sellers and the boys with their shoeshine boxes would rather listen to a good argument than earn a *drachma,* about three cents in U.S. money.

A breakwater encloses the sunny harbor where a few men are at work. One man is painting fresh bright lines around his boat. Another is working on his boat's motor. When night falls, his caique will be ready to tow a long line of small fishing boats, sometimes called *gri-gri* (gree-gree) boats, out to the fishing grounds.

Other men sit with their backs resting against a stone, mending their brown nets.

Back in the center of town, a street widens out into an open square called a *platia* (pla-tee′-a). The town hall, a fine two-story building, faces the platia. The school is usually nearby.

Across the square stands the church, often freshly plastered in light blue or white. The priest, wearing his long black robe and black stovepipe hat, strolls across the churchyard between the slender, dark green cypress trees. His beard is long, and he may have a bun of long hair tucked up under his hat. The priests of the Greek church follow the old custom of never cutting their hair.

Though towns are now lighted by electricity, tasks like netmending have not changed in many centuries.

The village priest is a familiar and important figure in the community.

Inside the church, some girls and women may be lighting candles. These they will leave burning before a picture of the Holy Mother and Child or before one of the many saints of the Greek church. They may bring other offerings on the festival day of a saint.

Girls and women like to visit the church or one of the small shrines on the hilltops. The girls and women do not have much social life except going to church or to the market.

If a girl wants more excitement, she may go to a big town to work in a factory, or she may go to Athens to work as a maid. She will work long enough to make up a dowry, the marriage gift most young men of Greece still expect.

The young men can always find friends to talk with, when they are not at work in the fields or out in boats. Toward twilight, most of the menfolk come to the village square, where small tables and chairs await them. There may be music from the bandstand. As the sad, wild tunes drift up the narrow streets, more villagers come strolling down to watch.

On holidays such as Easter and Christmas, all the townspeople gather at the square. People stroll in and out of the church or they may stay, sometimes standing, through a service that is three hours long.

Then comes the fun, for on holidays there is dancing in the square. The mayor himself may lead the long line, swaying in rhythm and circling the square; for he and the priest are the leading citizens.

The dancers either go hand in hand, or they hold opposite ends of twisted kerchiefs between them. Often one man leads the line with proud, high kicks, but the girls dance more gently, swaying from side to side and pointing their toes. These are the same steps that dancers of Greece have used for thousands of years.

Beyond the square, the road winds uphill and out into the countryside. Here women sit on the doorsills of their homes, embroidering and watching passersby. From inside a house comes the click of a loom as a woman weaves wool into brightly patterned cloth.

In the late afternoon, the soft jangle of bells sounds from up the hill road, as the flocks of goats come home for the night. The young herdsmen wave a greeting in passing.

The windows of the houses stand open, for the day is warm. If the house has two stories, the parlor is usually upstairs. This room has a row of chairs around its walls, a small table in the center of the room, and photographs of the mother and father are hung high on the walls.

Often there is an open porch where the family sits in the cool of the evening, listening to the sounds of the village, and perhaps to the music of a radio from a neighbor's home.

In many village homes, the kitchen is in a courtyard. If there is no running water, a large

Women prepare to follow the leader in a Greek dance.

tin can is hung upside down over the sink, with a faucet at its bottom. It is filled with water that is brought from a village well, perhaps on the back of a donkey.

Outdoors, there may be a round-topped, clay oven for baking bread.

The boys of the family keep up the woodpile, so there is fuel for cooking rice with bits of meat and raisins, or for dishes of eggplant and tomatoes cooked in olive oil. Festivals mean a feast of lamb, and once in a while there is goat meat. Small cubes of meat, browned on a skewer, are a favorite dish. Since many villages are near the sea, there may be fish to grill.

The boys, barefoot and with heads shaved, go fishing in tiny boats or play in the shallow pools along the shore.

Nearby, on the pebbly beach, their mothers and sisters may pound the family laundry clean at the edge of the waves, while the boys play about and fish. They sometimes catch a lobster or spear a small octopus.

"Nowhere," a Greek friend will tell you, "is the meat of the lobster so sweet and so tender as in Greece. And olives! You have not eaten the real olive until you have eaten it in Greece— the small, purple-black, bitter olive of the old grove near my home."

Olives, goat's milk cheese, and black bread make up many meals for village boys and girls.

A fisherman of the island of Spyros has a good catch.

Guests get special fare. For a visitor, first comes a spoonful of very sweet fruit jam, with a glass of water to wash it down.

"It is good water," the host will tell his guest, "fresh from the spring."

Then comes a very small cup of the thick coffee, which first came from Turkey long ago, and perhaps a bit of pastry.

Even to passersby, villagers like to offer some hospitality. It may be a handful of cherries, pale pink and freshly picked, or a bunch of grapes from nearby vines. A child may run out with a flower or a sprig of blossom from a fruit tree. It is always pleasant to greet a friend.

4. Letters from Tassos

Anastassios, whose nickname is Tassos, lives in a mountain village in the north of Greece, near the border of Yugoslavia. Life is changing in Greece, but on small farms and in remote villages life still moves in its old, more simple patterns. Tassos has an uncle and cousins who have moved to America. In these letters to his cousins we follow life in his small village through the cycle of a year.

September

Dear Cousins Yonni and Lena,

My mother, grandparents, and I send you greetings. We are keeping in good health, and hope you are too.

I am very happy, for our school teacher and

51

school mistress have just returned to the village. Two days ago our lessons started. The first day, the priest came to bless us, so that we will be good, honest, and obedient. My mother bought me new copybooks and two new school books. Soon we shall be very busy.

Your cousin,
Tassos

October

Dear Cousins,

Greetings! I am wondering how the weather is where you are living now. Here in the mountains it is autumn. The leaves of the trees have turned yellow and are falling. Already it is cold, and we are wearing our winter clothes. The stoves have been set up in the school.

Our teacher is giving us more lessons now. The work is harder this year. But I am working, and the teacher likes me.

We all send you greetings.

Tassos

November

Dear Cousins,

Greetings! So Yonni has become Johnny and Lena is Helen! You are now real Americans with your new names. I think your life must be different too, like your names.

Here in the mountains, winter has come. These days we see no sun. Already God has thrown us some snow.

You know how cold it is inside the house. I am glad to go to school in the morning. We have our prayers and then enter our classroom where the stoves are lighted.

The village children ask me if it snows in America. I tell them that snow does not fall there. Tell me if I am right.

Greetings from,

Tassos

December

Dear Cousins,

Mother, the grandparents, and I all send our kindest regards for Christmas.

The mountains around the village are white with snow now. The other day we school children climbed the mountain and cut down a pine tree.

When we got back to the school, we decorated the tree. Our teacher had collected money. Each child paid one drachma. The teacher went into town and spent the money on lights, ribbons, and toys. We have hung them all on the pine tree. It looks so beautiful now.

Soon it will be time for the big bonfire. You remember what fun that is. Two days before Christmas, all the village children will take wood from home to the village square. After the sun sets and it gets dark, all the people will gather. We will light the fire. And while the fire burns, all the boys and girls will sing and dance and have Christmas fun.

I am wondering what you will do for Christmas in America. Please let us know.

Tassos

January

Dear Cousins Johnny and Helen,

Here I am writing you, and I want to thank you very much for everything. We have received the Christmas parcels you sent. How happy we were!

The grandparents are so warm with the new blanket. How nice Mother looks in her new dress and new shoes! And you should have seen me during the holidays in the new clothes you sent to me. I looked like an American boy.

Very early on Christmas Day, the church bells rang. You remember how clearly they sound all over the village. I got out of bed and dressed in my new clothes and went to attend the service. I prayed to our Heavenly Father to protect us all.

When we left church, we found it had snowed. All of us children were so very happy, making snow balls. We had a very good time.

For the New Year, Mother made her New Year's cake. Into the cake, as you know, went a coin. When we cut the cake, the coin turned up in my slice. Since the person who finds the coin is the lucky one, I expect a very good year, with good reports in school.

I wish the same for you.

Tassos

February

Dear Cousins,

I write this letter to send you greetings, but I do not know when you will receive it. There has been so much snow! The roads have been blocked, and so no buses or lorries have been running. School was closed because of the cold weather. We stayed inside the house.

Now school has started again. All the students of the fifth and sixth grades of the Primary School took the examinations for the first half of the year. I am hoping for good marks.

Tassos

March

Dear Cousins,

I sit down again to visit with you. We have finished with Carnival now. We boys and girls dressed up in old or fancy clothes on that day, and we also wore masks. I did not even know Demetrios who lives next door, until we took off our masks.

Then, as you remember, came the start of the

long Lenten fast. But we need not wait for the feast of Easter for another chance to celebrate. Next week, on the 25th of March, we have our National Independence Day celebration.

In the morning, all of us children will march to church with our teachers. When the service is over, we shall go to school. We are decorating the schoolrooms now.

We will perform small plays and I will recite a poem. All the people of the village will come. I wish you could be here.

Tassos

April

Dear Cousins,

What a nice time we had at Easter! We were on vacation from school. On Good Thursday, before Easter, we boiled our eggs and dyed them red with beet juice. Then we went to the church to decorate the bier of our Lord Jesus.

On Saturday night, the bells of the church started ringing just before midnight. Mother, the grandparents, and I were ready. We were all wearing our best clothes. We each had a long yellow candle, and I had my red eggs.

How full the church was! The priest read the Gospel and chanted the *Christos Anesti,* "Christ Is Risen!" Then the light was passed from the priest's candle to all of the other candles and everyone went out into the square.

You may be sure I had some fireworks to set off. And we children started cracking the red eggs with one another. Do you do this in America? Do you have dancing for Easter, and some lamb roasted on a spit? I hope so.

Tassos

Late April

Dear Cousins,

So much good news! With the money your father sent, my mother has bought a donkey. What a good help that will be on the farm. Grandfather has also made a bargain for three goats. I shall tend them when school is out.

We are thinking very much of the farm these days. For now spring is really here. The swallows are back. I was the first child to see them this year, and had the fun of running to tell everyone in the village. Everyone is glad when the swallows come back, and the trees are green again.

Tassos

May

Dear Cousins,

These days we are having much rain. But last week the sun shone. Our teacher said, "Tomorrow we go on an excursion."

Mother prepared some bread and goat cheese for me. In the morning we all gathered with our teachers and started on our way. We walked high up into the mountains.

In the pine grove the ground was covered with flowers. Many birds were chirping, and we played games. When it was midday we sat down with our teachers and had our meal. The food was tasty and the water was cool. What a good time we had!

Tassos

June

Dear Cousins,

This month we have had our examinations in school. I have passed with good marks, and will graduate from Primary School. Only three children have stayed in the same grade. Now I am happy to have a nice rest from classes.

I shall be helping my mother in the fields. We have planted wheat, maize (corn), and potatoes this year. Mother cannot farm all of our land by herself, since Grandfather is now too old to work. She cultivates only seven *stremma* (one and three-quarter acres) of our fifteen stremma. When I graduate from school in three more years, I shall work on the farm. Then we shall grow more crops.

Now, when Mother does not need me in the fields and the goats do not need me in the pasture, I play ball with the boys and swim in the river. Do you have a river to swim in where you live?

Tassos

July

Dear Cousins,

I do not have much time to write, for it is the time of harvest. This year has been a worry. Some weeks ago we had an earthquake in the village. It shook the walls of some houses. The home of my friend Demetrios was one of them. The earthquake rang the church bells, too.

You know that we do not usually have summer rains. But this year we have had so much rain! These rains have kept us from harvesting and threshing until now. It is very warm these days, so we are busy in the fields.

Some of the villages on the plains below us bring in harvesting and threshing machines. But our fields are small, so we cut the crops by hand.

We thresh the grain with horses or oxen walking round and round the stalks. We scoop up the heads on flat shovels and fling them into the air to blow away the straw.

After the worry about the weather, it seems as though it will be a good harvest after all, and we are thankful for that.

Tassos

5. Of Gods and Men

The past is all around one in Greece. On almost every hilltop, roofless walls and columns of glowing marble are reminders of times long gone. Each ruin has a tale to tell, a tale of men and gods.

Greece was the first area of Europe where people learned to live together in towns with orderly rules to live by. These ancient Greeks made beautiful things and with eager minds they studied the world around them. They thought great thoughts and honored their gods.

Greek laws and government, their ways of

shaping buildings and of carving statues, their stories and ideas were so outstanding that we still admire and often follow them today.

Many people visit Greece each year to gaze at what is left of its splendid 2,500-year-old buildings and other works of art. They wander through the towns and countryside they have read about. They sail the island-dotted Aegean, as Greek sailors have done for thousands of years. They remember old tales of gods and men. Taking care of these tourists is now one of the important industries in Greece.

Let us look at some of the memorable gifts that ancient Greece has given to our world.

The City-States

The mountains of Greece divide the country into countless valleys, most of them facing the sea and cut off from one another by land.

In many of these seaboard valleys, harbor towns grew up. Farm villages dotted the slopes above, among the fields. Higher in the safety of the hills, small cities clustered around the palaces of local kings. On the high place of each city was its fortress, the *acropolis*. Each city with its nearby harbor town and farm villages made up an independent city-state.

In the earliest days of Greece these small city-states had kings. Down through the centuries, they tried many different kinds of government. Sometimes one man ruled the state. At other times, several men formed a council and ruled together.

Gradually, more and more of the men of the city-states became interested in government. They talked about their problems when they came to market. Speakers told their views. Then all the citizens of the state cast their votes on bits of broken pottery, since they did not have paper. We still use the Greek word, *democracy,* to describe this kind of government by the people. It was tried out and developed in Greece more than 2,500 years ago.

The city-states were small enough so that all the men who were citizens could gather to vote. This was necessary, for each man's views were important.

If a city grew too large, a few shiploads of people could be sent out to start a new town in some other land, or on an Aegean island. Greek towns sprang up throughout the Aegean Sea area. Others were founded on the shores of the Black Sea, in North Africa beside the Mediterranean Sea, in Sicily, and in distant Spain.

People in these new towns taught their young people the language and religion, the music and dances of their old homes. These Greek ways of living made up their civilization. Greek civilization spread to many lands as new colonies were settled.

Honor to the Gods

The most beautiful and strongly built buildings in every Greek town were the temples. For the early Greeks worshiped a whole family of gods and goddesses.

The gods and goddesses seemed very real to the people. The Greeks thought of the gods as having much the same feelings as humans. They were considered more powerful and more handsome than humans. And people believed that the gods lived forever.

It was Zeus, the father of the gods, who sent the thunder and lightning crashing and flashing through the sky. Ceres, the goddess of the earth, could make crops ripen well or shrivel on the stalk. Poseidon, the god of the sea, could send storms or fair winds. The ancient Greeks believed all these things.

There were a god of the sun and a goddess of the moon. The Greeks thought of them as a handsome youth and his beautiful twin sister, the son and daughter of Zeus. They had many powers, as did another daughter of Zeus, Athena. She was often honored as the goddess of wisdom.

Every town and city had a god or goddess watching over it, as Athena watched over her city of Athens. Every grove of trees had spirits living in it; the people thought of them as lovely maidens. Other spirit maidens who were called nymphs lived in the sea under the waves.

People honored these gods and spirits by building temples, at first of wood, with pillars made of tree trunks, later of stone. As time passed, the temples became more and more elegantly simple and beautiful in form.

The marble temples built by the Greeks 2,500 years ago have been copied in almost every great city of the western world. The beautiful figures of men and gods chiseled from blocks of marble

Pilgrims used to take offerings to hilltop temples.

in those far-off times are still studied and admired.

People tried to keep the gods and goddesses happy. They made offerings when they planted a field, when they started on a journey, or when they met together for a feast. They took gifts to the temples and the small shrines. Some took cocks, others took small figures molded of clay. Rich men sometimes took silver and gold.

Hundreds of people went to certain temples on pilgrimages. Almost every temple had special festivals when the people met for feasts and dancing.

69

Dancers wore costumes and masks and sang old songs. From these dances grew the idea of giving plays. Soon many cities had outdoor theaters where the people flocked to watch plays. Some were solemn stories of men and gods, others were very funny.

These theaters and plays were another gift from Greece to the world. Some of those ancient plays are still given in the open-air theaters of Greece today.

Storytellers told many tales of the gods and goddesses. They told of the lives of the gods at home among the clouds on top of Mt. Olympus and down in the world of men.

The storytellers were often musicians too. They strummed stringed lyres as they sang their stories. They were called minstrels.

It was many hundreds of years before those tales of the minstrels were written down. Some of them were so lovely or beautiful that they have lived on to this very day.

A minstrel named Homer is credited with putting together, about 800 B.C., many old tales into the very long, exciting story called "The Iliad." It tells about the Trojan War hundreds of years before—in about 1,200 B.C. Shiploads of warriors from many city-states on the mainland and islands of Greece had sailed away to fight a rich trading city of Asia Minor called Troy. For ten years they fought. At last they captured and burned the city. Then they sailed back to their homes with many captives.

Another story put together by Homer, full of marvelous adventures, is called "The Odyssey." It tells of the long journey home of some of the warriors, watched over by the gods.

A minstrel of old sings a long tale about the gods.

War and Peace

The city-states of Greece were so proud and independent that they often did not work well together. Sometimes, though, when they were all in danger, they joined together to face and fight the enemy.

One such time was the Trojan War. Hundreds of years after that war, in about 500 B.C., the Greek cities were again in danger—now from the powerful Persian Empire off to the east.

The armies of Persia conquered the Greek cities of Ionia in Asia Minor. For many years the people lived unhappily under Persian rule. Then they revolted.

The revolt angered the Persian emperor, who sent out a great army to stop it. When he had succeeded, he decided to conquer the homeland of Greece as well. Had he succeeded in that, he might have conquered all of Europe.

Once more the Greek states joined together. They fought bravely in some very bitter battles. The Persians invaded Greece more than once, by land and by sea. Sometimes the Greek cities were very near defeat. Athens lost most of its farmland. Even its Acropolis was bombarded from a nearby hill, and all of its beautiful temples were destroyed.

The city-states managed to drive off the soldiers and sailors from that great Persian Empire. These small democracies won a great victory against a mighty empire whose ruler thought he was a god.

Age of Greatness

When the Persian Wars were over, the ruler of Athens, a man named Pericles, decided to rebuild his city. He decided the temples on the Acropolis of Athens must be more beautiful than ever before.

Temples were built to the goddess Athena, to Nike the goddess of Victory, and to others. They were of such great beauty that people still come from afar to see them today, though the buildings are in ruins.

Pericles' time in Athens is still known as the Golden Age. Never in one small city have so many people created so much beauty and lasting worth. They built noble buildings, carved beautiful statues, shaped and painted lovely bowls and vases of clay. They played musical instruments, ran races, and played games. They sang songs, danced, and performed plays in large theaters.

A play called "The Wasps," written in the Golden Age of Greece, is presented in the old theater of Epidaurus.

They wrote beautiful poems and lively histories as well as plays.

Teachers gathered students around them and taught them to look at nature with care, and to think clearly. The words of some of these great teachers are still read and admired today.

Unfortunately, quarrels broke out among the city-states. These quarrels developed into war. By the time the war was over, the time of greatness was almost over, too, not only for Athens but for all the city-states of Greece.

A Greek God King

In the north, the king of Macedonia dreamed of uniting all Greece under his rule. He died as he was completing this project, but he passed on his dream to his son.

The son was a proud and brilliant prince named Alexander. He had a grander dream. He wanted to rule not only Greece but the world. Amazingly, he did make such a whirlwind conquest of most of the world he knew, that he is still called Alexander the Great.

Alexander died of a fever when he was still a

The ruined platform at left was the stage of this old Greek theater. The chorus danced in the center.

young man of 33. Already he had defeated Persia and had taken his armies across Asia to the borders of India. He had declared himself a god both in Greece and in Egypt. He had founded new cities named for himself in many lands. And he had planted the seeds of Greek civilization, its art and learning, throughout thousands of miles.

After Alexander's death, his empire was split between quarrelsome generals. But the civilization of the Greeks or Hellenes, as they called themselves, lived on in many lands.

Foreign Rule

After the time of Alexander, there were still artists and scholars in Greece, but there were no strong leaders. When other armies attacked, the Greeks could not resist them.

First came the Romans from the west. The men of Rome were much impressed by Greece. They built new temples and libraries and columned marketplaces in Greek cities. Back in Rome, they had built temples and statues in the Greek style. They took teachers home from Athens to teach the boys of Rome.

"The armies of Rome conquered Greece," it

76

A proud Roman temple lies in ruins near the foot of
the Acropolis in Athens.

has been said. "But the spirit of Greece conquered
Rome."

When the Roman Empire became so large that
it had to be divided, the eastern capital was set
up in the Greek city, Byzantium. Rome collapsed
in the west, some generations later. But the eastern
or Byzantine Empire continued for more than a
thousand years. It combined Greek, Roman, and
eastern ways, but its language and many of its
ways of living remained Greek.

As the Byzantine Empire's rule grew weaker,
invaders came from the west again. Frenchmen,

Germans, Florentines, and Venetians sailed into Greece. New fortress castles of small rulers from Europe grew up overlooking many a Greek harbor town from about A.D. 1000 to 1500.

The last of the Byzantine Empire, including Greece, was captured by the Turks in 1453. The Turks ruled Greece until 1830. Those were hard times for Greece. The cities and countryside were all under Turkish lords, and Athens dwindled to a village of huts.

Greeks have never liked being ruled by outsiders. For many years, though, they could only dream of freedom. The priests of the church helped to keep this dream alive.

At last in 1821 the Greeks rebelled. For ten years they fought. In 1830 Greece finally won its independence from the Turks.

Troubled Freedom

Slowly, with many struggles, the leaders began to build a new nation. Bit by bit during the next hundred years, more of the mainland and more islands again came under the government of Greece or Hellas, the Greeks' own name for their land.

In 1922, Greece and Turkey decided the best road to peace between them was to send home all the Turks from Greece and almost all the Greeks from Turkey. This was a bitterly difficult task, as many whole villages had to move from their old homes. The villagers marched long, slow, hungry miles to a "homeland" they had never seen.

More than a million people came "home" to Greece from Turkey. It was hard for them to find places to live and food to eat. It was difficult for the people of Greece to have so many new-comers arrive, many more than were leaving. There were some good businessmen and craftsmen among the newcomers, though. They brought carpet making, silk weaving, enamel working, and other industries new to Greece.

The country was just beginning to settle down when war came again. This was World War II. Again Greece was invaded, from the north, from the sea, and this time from the skies. Even after the war was over for most of the world, it continued in Greece as Communists tried to gain control.

During the past 20 years, with the support of

friendly countries, Greece tried to establish both a stable government and a strong economy.

A constitutional monarchy was established after World War II. A parliament was elected then, too, to make the nation's laws. Twenty years after the establishment of this government, however, there was still political unrest in Greece. The struggle continues for a government that has the support of the many differing groups of Greek people.

People in cities and villages alike are interested in government and politics. They read newspapers eagerly and discuss the news of the day. Because their feelings about their country are intense, these discussions sometimes rise to shouts. The spirit of those long-ago city states that gave democracy to the world is still very much alive.

6. The Domes of Byzantium

A New Faith

A man with burning eyes and a ringing voice walked on foot from town to town in Asia Minor. In every town he gathered people around him and preached to them about a new religion. He told of one loving, all-powerful God who sent His Son to earth as Jesus the Christ, to teach men how to live together.

This man was called Paul. The new religion he taught was the religion of Christ—Christianity.

Many of the people of Greece turned to the new religion. Many temples of the old gods and goddesses were turned into Christian churches. The greatest temple of Athens, the Parthenon, had been dedicated to Athena, but it too became a Christian church, dedicated to Mary, Mother of Jesus.

As time went by, the Christians honored especially good and holy people, whom they called saints. They believed that after death these saints would be close to God in heaven, where they would try to help people who asked for help through prayer.

People took offerings to the new churches as they had to the old temples. They prayed to God and to the saints, much as they had formerly asked the old Greek gods and goddesses for help.

The Byzantine Church

About three hundred years after Christ lived, His teachings became the state religion of the whole Roman Empire. About the same time, the Roman Empire was divided in half, because it was too big to be ruled from one city.

The Church was divided too, hundreds of years later, into eastern and western branches. The western branch was called the Roman Catholic Church. The eastern branch was called the Eastern

Orthodox Church. Greece belonged to the Eastern Roman Empire, and later followed the Eastern Orthodox Church.

The capital of the Eastern Empire was the Greek city of Byzantium, so it was called the Byzantine Empire. Long after the name of the city was changed to Constantinople, the empire was still called Byzantine.

After Rome fell, western Europe faced many dismal years called the Dark Ages. The Byzantine royal court, however, helped to keep learning and art alive in the Christian world. This Byzantine Empire lasted for more than a thousand years. Both empire and church were ruled from their capital city of Constantinople.

In many parts of Greece, churches built under the Byzantine Empire can still be seen, usually topped with domes. Many are whitewashed on the outside and richly decorated inside with glowing wall pictures called mosaics done with bits of colored marble or glass.

Tucked away, often on hilltops that are hard to reach, one can also still find monasteries and nunneries. The monks and nuns who lived in them were men and women who had decided to give their lives to God. They moved off into quiet places apart from the world. A few monks and nuns still live in those old buildings today.

The branch of the Christian Church that is the state religion of Greece today is still called the Eastern or Greek Orthodox Church. At its head is a leader called the patriarch, and under him are bishops.

The bishops choose from each village a man to act as priest. Often the village priest has not had much more schooling than the other villagers. He has a wife and family and lives like his people, perhaps doing a little farming. He is an important man, for the church has a voice in government and education as well as in religious life.

The church services of the Eastern or Greek Orthodox Church are called masses. They are very long, often lasting about three hours. All the people come to church to worship, especially on Christmas, Easter, the Feast of the Assumption of the Virgin, and on the festival day of the local saint.

Often when there is no service, villagers will stop at a church or shrine to light a candle or to say a prayer.

7. The Luck of St. Cassianus

Condensed from the tale as told by Alan J. B. Wace

Perhaps because for many hundreds of years ancient Greeks thought of their gods and goddesses as almost human friends, Greeks of today do not think it is sacrilegious or disrespectful to make a little joke, such as this, about saints whom they honor and about life in heaven. This story suggests the way in which religious beliefs have become a warm, friendly part of everyday life.

Back in the days when strange things came true, there once lived a sly fellow. He could always think of a trick to get what he wanted in the world. If it was not strictly honest, he did not mind.

When the end of his life drew near, he began

to think about Heaven. He knew that his record on earth was not very good. He would not be likely to get a ticket to enter the gates of Paradise. So he made a ticket for himself, printing it very carefully, and he kept it close at hand.

When the day came, he made his way to the gates of Paradise. An angel was on guard there, and the sly fellow presented his ticket to the angel. The angel did not look at it closely, and so he was admitted.

The sly fellow entered Paradise, and started to walk up the main road, paved with shining marble. But he did not feel happy. He longed for a friend.

On his right he saw a beautiful large café, even larger and grander than those near Constitution Square in Athens. Such a grand café would never be found on earth! Its walls were hung with great mirrors; its polished floor was as smooth and shining as another mirror. Large soft sofas of red plush stood against the walls, and on a marble counter could be seen a marvelous array of cakes, rich with cream and chocolate.

The tables inside the café and outside on the sidewalk were crowded with well-dressed, well-fed saints. The sly fellow felt that he would not fit in there, so he looked around for a simpler place.

On the other side of the road was another café. Its windows were small and two panes were broken and pasted over with brown paper. Its mirrors were spotted, its tables were shaky. Flies wandered over the few cakes on its dirty marble counter.

There was only one customer, a sad and shabby saint who sat alone at a chipped table.

The sly fellow felt more at home here. He stepped up to the table where the sad saint sat and greeted him.

"Good day," said the saint in reply.

"What news?" asked the sly fellow.

"So-so," said the saint. "Do sit down and have something."

When a waiter came, after a long wait, the sly fellow ordered a lemonade.

"It is all gone," said the waiter.

So the sly fellow had to be content with a cup of coffee—muddy coffee at that.

"Why do you sit here alone?" he asked the saint. "Why do you not sit with St. Nicholas, St. George, St. Demetrius, and St. Basil and the others at the fine big café across the way?"

"Don't you know who I am?" asked the saint with a sigh.

"No, I am afraid I do not," said the sly fellow.

"I am St. Cassianus," was the answer.

"St. Cassianus," the sly fellow repeated. "I do not understand."

"You see," said the sad saint, "my festival is on February 29th, so I get offerings only every fourth year. That is why I cannot afford to go to the other café. All the other saints have festivals every year and get many offerings."

The sly fellow saw a chance to play one of his tricks.

"You must sue a rich saint—St. Nicholas, for instance. He should give you an allowance of so many measures of oil and so many candles every year. Then you too could live in style."

The sad saint was finally persuaded by his new friend. The sly fellow drew up a claim for him; St. Cassianus presented it before St. Peter as judge. St. Peter glanced through it.

"Hm," he said. "Did you draw up this claim all by yourself?" He looked sternly at the sad and kindly saint.

"Well, I did have a little help from a man I met at a café," the saint admitted.

"Where is he?" asked St. Peter, and the sly fellow was called.

St. Peter took one look at him.

"Where is this fellow's ticket to Paradise?" he asked. The angel at the gates went hunting through the records to find it.

After one glance at the ticket, St. Peter tore it to bits. "He made this himself," he said. "Throw him out."

So the angel police threw the sly fellow out of Heaven. He had no ticket for Hell, so he could not enter there either. But outside, between Heaven and Hell, is a small boatman's café. There he sits forever with a few like him, who have no place to go. It was there I met him, and that is how I am able to tell you this tale.

8. Life in Athens

"When I grow up," say boys all over Greece, "I will go to Athens. That is where life can be enjoyed. That is where one always has coins in his pockets."

Athens is indeed a lively city. It has one-quarter of all the factories in Greece, and about one-quarter of the country's people live in or near the city. They know that the best wages are paid there.

The headquarters of all the principal businesses are in Athens. It also has a large university. There are fine shops and stores, cafés and restaurants, theaters, and many, many hotels.

Athens is the capital city of Greece, the seat of the government and home of the king. The National Parliament meets in Athens. The country is divided into prefectures, similar to states. The governments of the prefectures are run from Athens or run by men sent out from the capital city. The free public schools of Greece, even those in the smallest village, are also run from Athens. They are attended by boys and girls from six to fourteen. Many people in other towns and cities think that there is too much control from Athens!

Airlines, railroads, highways, and steamship lines of Greece all fan out from Athens. Many, many visitors flock to Greece to visit beautiful old ruins of temples, theaters, and market places, the scenes where the Golden Age once flourished. Since Athens was the heart of ancient Greece, visitors are sure to make it the center of their stay.

Just as the life of the country centers at the capital, the life of the city itself centers around Constitution Square. At one side of the square stretches the old palace, which now houses the parliament. On the other sides rise tall, modern buildings housing offices and hotels.

The paved part of the square is covered with small painted iron tables and chairs. At twilight the chairs fill with members of families and groups of friends. Waiters from the cafés fronting on the square hurry back and forth with pastries and small cups of coffee, with lemonade or frosty dishes of ice cream.

Peddlers stroll by, calling their wares. Some have huge bunches of sponges bouncing like balloons at their shoulders. Others have baskets filled with packets of pink-shelled pistachio nuts in small twists of paper.

A sponge seller on Athens' Constitution Square offers wares brought from the bottom of the sea.

As shops and offices close in the tall, new buildings rising around the square, more people join the crowds. Some stroll on the fragrant, shady paths of the wooded gardens behind the old palace.

Buses chug to a stop to pick up the waiting passengers. Then they roar away again as taxi brakes screech and drivers honk their horns. Voices rise and the city hums with lively noise.

It is not only Constitution Square that is lively. There are many squares scattered around the city, and each one, large or small, has its cafés, its small tables under trees, its gatherings of friends.

"Half the business of the country is conducted in the coffee shops," say the Greeks with a smile.

The people of Athens have long days. They are up early in the morning, and after a light breakfast start off to school or work. At noon, they go home for lunch and a nap which is especially welcome in the heat of summer days. Shops, offices, and all businesses close for the midday hours.

As the first cool breaths of afternoon breeze steal over the city, people stir again. Shops and offices reopen, to stay open until eight or eight-thirty in the evening. The cafés come to life as ladies gather for tea at six or seven o'clock, and men from offices meet to talk about business or politics.

It is not until nine in the evening, or even later, that people think of their evening meal. Most of the time they eat this meal at home, which for most city people is an apartment rather than a house. For special occasions, the family goes out to a taverna or restaurant.

In the winter and chilly spring, dinner is served inside at the tavernas. Most of them are rather small, with floors of stone, and smooth oilcloth covers on the tables. The rooms are warm and perhaps a bit smoky from cooking, but they are full of music and laughter.

In many tavernas, diners may choose their food from the huge copper pans in the nearby kitchen, as the cook lifts the lids. There will be rice pilaff, with bits of meat; lamb with beans; grape leaves stuffed with rice and meat; fish freshly grilled; and perhaps lobster and octopus, also fresh from the sea. There will be salad of tomatoes, herbs and greens, and olives, of course. For sweets, rice pudding will be offered, or pastry dripping with honey and crunchy with sesame seeds.

94

It is dining out-of-doors in summer that people like best. Then almost every taverna moves its tables outside. There may be only a small paved courtyard, but it is open to the stars, and to watchers from the apartments all around. People may sit on their balconies to enjoy the fun.

Tables may also be set out on a flat roof, with crepe paper flowers nodding on trellises. Singers and perhaps a musician with a mandolin will wander among the tables. Everyone may join in a favorite song. Above them, the lighted marble temples still standing on the Acropolis remind one of the Golden Age of Greece. They seem to float in the night sky.

Perhaps the whole family, rich or poor, drives out to the country for a breath of cool air. If they do not have a car, a shared taxi, a bus, or even a truck will do.

Some take a picnic to eat on a rocky beach; others visit one of the big garden restaurants on the hill slopes in the suburb of Kifissia. Or they choose one of the many small restaurants that line the Bay of Phaleron, where the stars dip down to the waves and twinkle to the music of the fiddle and mandolin.

Tavernas line the slope of the Acropolis in Athens.

For entertainment in the summer, there are plays given out-of-doors, at the old theater built by a Roman emperor on the slope of the Acropolis. Most of the people enjoy visiting friends or singing or dancing. They may go to the movies, of course, or even watch a shadow puppet show with flat old leather puppets behind a lighted screen, though these have become rare.

When the night begins to cool, home they go. But homes in Athens can be hot at night in the summer. Many families throw open the windows and lean out into the night air, until at last it is cool enough to sleep.

Of course, life in Athens is not all fun and frolic. Housewives take their shopping bags in the morning and head for the busy open food markets. One row of shops or stands sells fruits, another vegetables, a third meats. There are special fish markets and others for dry, packaged groceries, so shopping takes a good deal of time.

Young people go off early in the morning to their schools, with heavy schoolbags. They take their schoolwork seriously. If they wish to go to a gymnasium to prepare for college, they must pass an examination at the end of the sixth grade. Those who do not get very good grades go on to other schools to train for work in offices, factories, and for other kinds of jobs.

Men and women line up for buses that take them to their offices or factories, shops or hotels. These city workers make more money than do workers in smaller towns and villages, and they like living in Athens, the lively heart of Greece.

9. The Bottom of the Sea

Alexandros whistled as he watched the sponge divers unload their catch. Under the mass of slimy sponges lay three big clay jugs. In olden times such jugs had been used for storing oil or wine. But these jugs had not held wine or oil for many years. They were crusted with lime and seashells, like the rocks at the bottom of the sea.

Alexandros longed for a better look. The shape of the jugs was just like those his Uncle Lambis had showed him last summer. They had been in the workroom of the archaeological dig where Uncle Lambis had been in charge. Most of them were in pieces, but student workers were fitting pieces together like rounded jigsaw puzzles.

"Some nice old *amphorae*," Uncle Lambis had said then. "It was probably not long after the Trojan War that the storekeeper of this old palace lined these jugs up neatly in the storeroom. Then there apparently was a big fire in the palace. See all the blackened spots. We've found remains of charred beams up at the palace site, too. The roofs fell in, and the palace was abandoned.

"Now, nearly 3,000 years later, we have come to dig into the ruins. And here are the old jugs, waiting to tell us their story."

That whole scene flashed into Alexandros' mind as he spotted the shell-encrusted jugs. "Could these be valuable too?" he wondered.

"Where did you find those?" he asked the divers.

The sponge divers darted quick glances at him. They did not speak. They did not want to give away the location of good sponge beds. So they did not talk much to strangers. Alexandros, whose friends called him Aleco, did not belong here, they knew. He was not an island boy, but was

Aleco's holiday island has a fine sandy beach.

here from Athens on a holiday with his family.

The sponge divers turned their backs on Aleco. One stooped and threw an old canvas over the jugs. Then they went on spreading the sponges on the pebbles of the beach to dry.

Aleco shrugged and strolled away down the beach toward the inn where he and his family were staying. He hadn't yet unpacked his fins and snorkel, for he had come down for a look at the beach first. After seeing those old jugs, he was eager for a look at the sea bottom. Perhaps he could discover some old relics on his own.

That evening at dinner, Aleco told his father about the strange, shell-encrusted jugs. The inn where the family stayed had no dining room.

The guests took their meals in the town, at sidewalk tables outside small tavernas. Aleco's father brushed a pink blossom from his plate as he listened. It had fallen from a bush beside their table.

Aleco's father was a busy lawyer in Athens. It bothered him that his son did not like to study and found schoolwork dull. All he seemed to care for were swimming and snorkeling.

"Hm," said the father thoughtfully, as Aleco talked excitedly on. "Let's walk around by way of the beach on our way back to the inn. Let's take another look at these jugs, these old amphorae, if that is what they are."

"Fine!" said Aleco. "I guess Uncle Lambis would be surprised if I turned up a real find."

He had not forgotten his uncle's scorn when his last grades from school had come.

Sending Mother and Aleco's sister Irena back to the inn, Aleco and his father set out for the beach. It was easy enough to locate the small boat of the divers. The sponges were still drying on the pebbles nearby. The old canvas still lay beside the boat, just as the men had tossed it over the jugs. But when Aleco lifted it gently, there was nothing under it but pebbles. The strange old jugs were gone.

"Hm," said Father. "That is odd. Well, we'll take a look around town tomorrow morning."

Next morning the two set off for the market.

"Let's take a short cut," Father suggested, "through the old town."

A few steps down led them from the street level into the remains of a city of 2,000 years ago. Archaeologists had dug away the topsoil that had covered it through the centuries. They had found well-paved streets.

One street led across the area straight to the modern market section. It led past doorways of small houses that had vanished long ago. The roofs and most of the walls were gone, but the floor plans were clear. Here and there a bit of wall remained. Some bits had plaster still on them, even traces of bright pictures that had been painted on the plaster.

Father stopped at one of the doorways and pointed inside.

"See the clay counter there?" he asked. "That may have been the sales counter of a shop in long-ago times. Those jugs that were lost at sea may have been headed for a shop like this one."

"What I want to know," said Aleco, "is where they were headed for last night."

"Have patience," said his father. And on they strolled.

In the market lanes, Father poked along, looking at the sandals hanging in front of one shop, sampling the grapes at another. He stopped to visit with all the shopkeepers, laughing at their jokes. Aleco shifted from one foot to the other. What a waste of time this seemed! But Father's eyes were busy.

They turned a corner down a narrow lane shaded partly with awnings and partly with vines trained across the lane overhead. Father whistled softly. Aleco followed his gaze. In the shadows at the doorway of a shop, beneath dangling donkey bells, lay three big lime-crusted jugs.

"So you want a donkey bell?" said Father, to Aleco's surprise. "This shop seems to have the best selection. Let's take a look."

It was only when they had chosen one bell and bargained until they got it for half the shopkeeper's price that Aleco's father said, "What are the jars back there?"

"Just some old things," the shopkeeper said with a vague wave of his hands. "Very old, maybe. I don't know." He looked uneasy.

"Interesting," said Aleco's father. "I would give you a few drachmas for one."

The shopkeeper's eyes brightened. He loved to bargain. It was some minutes before the two agreed on a price. Then Aleco went off with the big jug cradled in both arms.

"Now we have one of the jugs," said Aleco. "If you think that it is really old, I'll go out snorkeling to hunt for the spot it came from."

"The Aegean Sea is a big pond to start hunting in, without any clues," his father smiled. "This does look really old, though. I think we'll write Uncle Lambis about it right away."

Aleco felt like running back to the inn, to get that letter written. But he had to watch his footing, with the precious jug in his arms.

The two were almost at the inn door before they noticed a broad-shouldered man hurrying down the road toward them, waving.

"Lambis!" cried Aleco's father. "Just the fellow we want to see."

"Uncle Lambis!" echoed Aleco. "See our find!"

Soon the three were seated in the inn garden, studying the jug.

"It looks good," Lambis agreed. "About two thousand years old, I'd guess."

Aleco and his family ate at this outdoor restaurant.

"Two thousand years under water?" Aleco
cried.

"I think an old trading ship loaded with jugs
of wine or oil sank in the waters between here
and Turkey," Uncle Lambis said. He nodded
out to sea where the Turkish shore was visible.

"Sponge divers began bringing in jugs like this
a few years ago, over in Turkey. After a while,
some archaeologists got the divers to show them
the spot where they had found the jugs. Sure
enough, there was the wreck of a ship."

"But after years under water," said Aleco,
"was there much left?"

"Not much wood was left," Uncle Lambis said.
"But the clay jugs were there, lined up just as
they had been packed in rows on the ship. There
were some coins, too, and tools and other things
that had belonged to the sailors."

"But how—?" Aleco started to ask.

"I'll show you how underwater archaeologists
work if you will help me make friends with the
sponge divers," smiled Uncle Lambis. "As it
happens, I have been doing some diving this
summer. I'm eager to get into this new field
of underwater archaeology."

Aleco wasted no time. When they all went down to the taverna for lunch, he spoke to the friendly young waiter.

"Do you know any sponge divers?" he asked.

"My brother is one. He is the best," said the waiter proudly. He turned to Aleco. "I think you spoke to him yesterday on the beach. He has told me."

"We'd like to have a business talk with him," said Aleco's father. "Could you arrange it?"

The waiter looked more serious. "I will see," he said, giving the table top an extra polish.

When they returned for dinner that evening, the young waiter's eyes were sparkling.

"My brother will meet you, sir," he said. "I have told him you are a big man from Athens and very kind."

So it happened that later that evening Aleco, feeling very grown up, sat with his father and Uncle Lambis at a small table in a waterfront café bright with electric lights. There was loud, lively music from a radio. The young brother of their waiter friend sat with them. At first he just sipped his coffee and listened. Soon he was talking as excitedly as the rest.

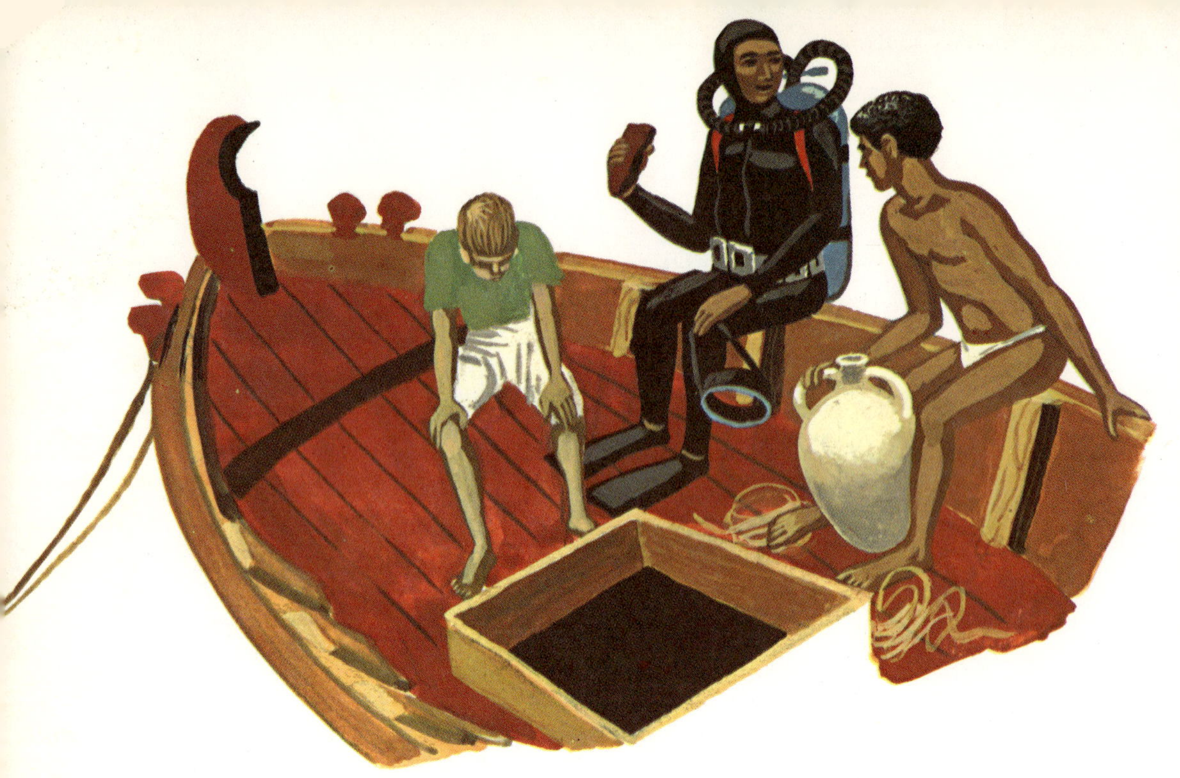

A few days later, Aleco and Uncle Lambis stood with the young sponge diver at the rail of a caique out at sea. Uncle Lambis had an air tank on his back. He was dripping wet.

The sponge diver wore just a loin cloth. He was dripping too.

"There is a ship there," said Uncle Lambis. "It was a good-sized ship, I should say. There do not seem to be many jars, so I think it was a different kind of ship. By just poking around, I found this old ax head."

He showed Aleco a lump of metal, so coated

that it was almost shapeless. But it did have a hole where a wooden handle had been fitted on.

"May I go down?" begged Aleco. "Just once?"

"Not without practice." Uncle Lambis shook his head. "It's too deep here. This won't be like snorkel fishing."

"When will you start work?" Aleco asked. "I'll practice."

"Not until next summer at least," Uncle Lambis said. "This kind of exploring takes a lot of planning and money. We must make arrangements with the government. Then we will have to set up a camp, hire boats, and bring more diving equipment and cables to lift heavy finds. Underwater cameras will be needed to photograph the whole site and keep track of where things are found."

"May I work for you next summer?" Aleco begged.

"I think perhaps we could find a place for a young man who was studying very hard," said Uncle Lambis.

"O, how I will study!" cried Aleco. "I'm going to learn to be a great archaeologist, and explore the bottom of the sea."

About the Author

Jane Werner Watson has visited Greece five times, for stays totaling several months. She and her husband have sailed among the islands and have flown or driven over the mainland of Greece, ranging from the island of Corfu in the west to Rhodes in the east, and from Macedonia in the north to southerly Crete.

The Watsons have visited the ruins of the homes of such Trojan War heroes as Menelaus of Sparta, Agamemnon of Mycenae, King Nestor of Pylos, and Achilles, whose home was near Volos, a modern port. They have also visited the ruins of Troy itself.

Present-day Greece and its hospitable people have interested the Watsons as much as its glamorous past. They have been guests in homes both rural and urban, prosperous and simple. From all these experiences comes this book to join other Garrard titles by Jane Watson on India, Iran, Ethiopia, Thailand, Nigeria, Peru, and Egypt.

ITALY
YUGOSLAVIA
ALBANIA
Tassos' home
Macedonia
Salonika
Mt. Olympus
home of gods
GREECE
Corfu
home of Achilles
home of Odysseus
(Ulysses)
Ithaca
Athens
Corinth
Piraeus
Canal
Jonian
Mycenae
home of
Agamemnon
Sea
Peloponnesus
Sparta
home of
Menelaus
Pylos
home of
Nestor